Sales Mastery Made Easy
Selling Secrets Revealed

Kishore K Muralidharan

Table of Contents

Contents

Foreword	4
Life's First Sales Pitch	5
Seller in me	7
What to sell	8
Selling an Art	10
Talk more to sell more	11
Why sell	12
Who sells	13
Who will trust you?	14
You or Brand	15
Brand or product	165
Emotional buying	17
Ego satisfaction	187
Buy for need	20
Buy for fun	21
Addicted Buyer	23

Customer is important	24
Qualified to Sell	25
Knowledge and salesman	26
The Canvas	28
Trigger to Senses	30
Buyer, Seller, and Product	31
Modern E Tools	30
The first date	31
Don't give them what you have	34
Objections are welcome	36
Not to sell	37
Time management	39
Energy in sales	40
Understand Trend	41
The customer expectations	42
Door to Door Selling	43
Industrial Selling	45
FMCG selling	46
Pharmaceutical Selling	48
Dealer sales	51
BB Matrix- The Buyer Behaviour	53
Diamonds	54
Power Horse	55
Champions	57
Deep Mine	58

Foreword

A Salesman or a marketing official is a link between the producer company and the buyer/customer. He is primarily an advertiser of his company's products/services. Unlike other advertisers, the salesman is tasked with bringing income for the producer company. In achieving this he talks to the prospect, educates him by comparing products/services of other companies, and ultimately tempts his prospect to buy his product/service and generates income for his company.

Selling is not an easy task. There is a lot of difference between selling a product and selling a service. For selling a laptop the salesman can display a laptop and show its features. But how would you explain the benefits of term insurance that comes only after the death of the buyer? There is no model to display. Service marketing is a subject by itself

There is no uniform code to be followed by salesmen in all situations, except honesty and a positive attitude. There are as many methods as there are products/services. A newspaper is a product that is different every day, only the name continues. Is selling technique is unique. In the Hotel business, the salesman sells room-space, in airlines, it is space marketing, in the TV channel, it is time-marketing. Every situation is different for a salesman.

That does not mean one should not learn about selling at all. For a busy salesman, an easy-to-read-handbook on sales and salesman-like Dr Muralidharan's Sales Mastery Made Easy is recommended for it offers an easy reading that may be undertaken even during travel. The book, though short and simple chapters, takes you through a plethora of concepts and situations without making you feel bored. Sales, you will agree with me, is an elevating task.

Dr.V.N.S.Pillai

Author: Pension & Annuity, Economics from the Scriptures

Life's First Sales Pitch

The history of sales cannot be determined, because the sales process is as old as the human race. It should not be a surprise if I say every living being on this planet gets involved in the sales process, without even them being aware of this.

Let's see when we started the first sale of our life. How many of us must have started this process while we were in the womb? It may sound weird and crazy, but the truth is we did our sales right from the time we were in the womb.

The happiest time of a pregnant woman is when she starts to feel the movement of the child in her, she gets delighted each time the baby makes a move. It is nature's way of attracting attention to the baby. This builds a bond between the mother and the unborn child.
I would say that the first move of the baby in the womb is the first and the best sales pitch.

This process continues till the time the baby is born, this is how nature ensures a strong bond. Once the baby is born, its first cry is another strong sales pitch. Its respiration gets normal. The mother feeds the baby and a very strong relationship begins.

This is true with all living beings, the baby ensures that they get proper care from their mother through their cry or other attention-seeking methods.

Our relationship with sales begins much before we could realise. Every day we do so many transactions and interactions, which has some benefit for exchange. Nature too lures us with various sales strategies. We get attracted to the beauty of a Rose, the delicious and colorful strawberries and thus the story of sales goes on.

Seller in me

'Salesman' is a forbidding word. The sales profession is rarely an option for MBAs and most of the successful salesmen joined the profession by accident and they have now no regrets. Sales as a process are very interesting, and we all are part of this process. Knowingly or unknowingly we are salespersons every day. We sell ideas to our colleagues, friends, family, customers, and many more people; we convince our kids why vegetables are good, we make our spouses agree to dine in a particular restaurant, in all these activities selling happens.

Every day at least forty times we enter into the selling process. Selling is something we need not be upset about, it is as natural as breathing.

The moment we want another person to accept our view or idea or request, we are engaged in the selling process. We make the other person comfortable enough to accept our offer. It is the same activity the salesman does, he makes you comfortable and helps you realise the need for his product. This is another dimension of selling, marketing. Observe the life insurance Salesman who convinces you to purchase his product/service even without your seeing a 'specimen of the product'. You will happily accept his product in exchange for some of your hard-earned money. This means that there is a seller in each one of us.

What to sell

In our personal lives, we are very much involved in selling. From the time we get out of our bed we are busy trying to satisfy our different needs - first, the bed coffee we have is a need-satisfaction process. To give us this feeling the coffee company must have enticed us into buying their product and having satisfied us it has made its way into our life.

Your wife is sold the idea that you will feel good with coffee of a specific brand. You must have initially convinced her of your liking for the coffee that keeps you going energetic all through the day. Once out of bed you need coffee in the morning and this need of yours is addressed by your wife because she was convinced with your idea of the morning nectar and she readily became the subscriber of your idea. Here she gives you the best-brewed coffee to keep you in good humor and energetic. She may even get a smile in return.

This example gives us an idea as to how we get involved in selling each day.

Anything and everything can be sold. Won't you agree? Everyone lives by selling something says the American Marketing Association. We are always engaged in the selling process. Many find it difficult to accept this selling process because they don't see money in every transaction. It's because they believe that in all selling finance is involved.

When a service is exchanged for another service, there happens a selling. There is Negotiation at times. The value of a service is perceived and so does the exchange value. Just imagine a situation, where we are asked for a donation by an orphanage and we give Rs 1000 for their cause, is it a selling process? Let's analyse the situation, who is selling what or what is that being exchanged, guess who gets what in this transaction.

The orphanage that receives the donation is benefited as their need is satisfied. We feel good for doing this charity. Here charity is sold as a service in exchange. The donors too got what they wanted. This is a pure service sale that took place. Both parties are happy with this transaction.

Selling an Art

It is often confusing whether selling is science or art. Many people believe that selling skills are God-given and not everybody's cup of tea. Most people refrain from this profession for the fear of failure and the humiliation of rejection. In sales, the new entrants have to learn to live with rejection. The method of learning through trial and error takes a long time in giving mastery over a skill.
Scientific sales training can reduce this duration of learning through experience. Selling is an art that can be taught. There are many proven methods designed to make
the selling process easy. Once we learn this skill we can be more successful in selling.

The quality that is needed to become a successful sales professional is 'attitude'. An attitude of perseverance. Many people shy away from this profession because they find it difficult to accept failure. A successful sales professional would never give up his mission midway; he is prepared to face any failure head-on. Once he is convinced of the presence of a need in a customer he works hard to take the mission to its logical conclusion.

Talk more to sell more

It is a myth that only talkative people are good at selling. Do you agree with this?

Selling is a scientific process involving many steps and direct interactions with the customer are just one of these steps.

The skill needed for a successful sale is to understand the customer, his needs, wants, and aspirations. These should be developed once the sales professional understands the customer. He should be able to offer an answer to the customers' needs. The sole objective of the salesman should be to satisfy his customer's requirements with the features offered by his products or service.
No amount of talking will help in selling the products unless the current customer finds it exciting to buy.

The product or service should be able to address the customer's need and that too at a price he is willing to pay. Smart salesman helps his customers tide over financial challenges through proper advice on the availability of funds or lease arrangements. Any good sales organisation has a proper liaison with Finance Companies willing to finance their products/services. We see such examples in real estate, automobiles, tour operators, etc. It is not only the sales talk but many other factors influence in the sales.

Why sell

Selling is a process in which a need, desire, or want is satisfied, each day we get involved in this process because there is always some need to be satisfied. Since we are aware of the existence of this process, it is always better to equip ourselves with the appropriate skill. In sales there is always an exchange of product/service, sometimes even emotional gratification can be part of a sales exchange. The child becomes happy when it is offered a toffee, here a toffee is exchanged for happiness. An employee is promoted for his good work, appreciation was given in recognition of his good job done.

The sales process should have positive outcomes. 'Reprimand' cannot become part of the selling process because here both the employee and employer are dissatisfied and thus it is a negative outcome for the process. The sales process always involves positive activities which should have a feel-good factor built into them.

Who sells

The sales profession is not restricted to seasoned professionals who are trained to sell. This is one of the old professions which happened even much before trading came into existence.

Even when money did not evolve sales did take place in the form of barter. Then also the one who could present his product well was a gainer in barter. In that era too our ancestors must have sold their service in exchange for produce, they shared their hunt with all those who participated in hunting, shared the meat.

There must have been a negotiation on who gets the best portion of the meat, the person who convinced others about his skill better would have got the best part of the meat.

Anybody who has any product or service at his disposal which he or she could exchange for something else, which they want in return participate in the selling process and he becomes the seller. If we go with such an understanding then we would be surprised to note that every one of us is a salesperson.

The person, who understood the sales process better, will always sell more than those who are unprepared.

Who will trust you?

Trust is a quality sales professional should consciously develop. Every successful sales professional is standing strong on the foundation of trust he has built over years. A trustworthy salesperson would be able to sell his product at a premium; the premium price is for the guarantee provided by his credibility.

This is exactly the reason why people pay a premium price to trusted brands like Apple, Sony, Mercedes Benz, etc. Every organisation in the product or service business work very hard to build its credibility and brand image, for which they spend a lot of money. As an individual, it may not be possible to spend big money in building one's brand, but you cannot stay away from building your image as trustworthy sales professional. The only successful way forward is working on certain values and principles. You should have solid values which you should never compromise and these values would create your image and thus you should be able to become a branded salesperson, whom your customers can depend upon. Think about it; are you on the right track? Are you a brand?

You or Brand

Why should a customer buy from you? Is it you the reason for their purchase or is it the brand that offers them confidence and comfort?

Most often we would find that the brand is responsible for the customers' buying decisions. Is it possible to change the attitude of your customers? Can someone just buy a product because of you or can you be the reason for their purchase? This is a million-dollar question every salesperson should ask himself. It is a difficult and unpleasant question because we are not used to difficult and negative results. The best way to prevent a negative answer is to avoid asking tough questions. This one question would give you an insight into your position as to what you hold.

As sales professionals, we should agree that these days product quality and brand image alone cannot help in decision making, because most of the product or service organisations are consciously building their brands and these brands compete with others in terms of quality and brand promotions.

The only difference that can help your customers decide is 'you'; the brand called you.

Brand or product

The market is full of products and many of them are generic and have no identity of their own. The identification of a product carried was the source from where the product was procured, for example, Shimla Apple, Fuji Apple, a Swiss watch, Scotch whisky, Dehradun basmati rice, etc.

In many cases, the source of the product was seen as its standard of quality. It was much later that brands started evolving to create an individual identity for each product, there could be Many kinds of whisky produced in Scotland and they wanted to have a different identity for each product from the different distillery.

Today every product has many different brands and each of these brands carries unique features that differentiate them from its rivals. Gone are the days when quality was the only concern because quality is no longer a differentiating factor as it is a minimum requirement for any product to be in the market. The customer buys a product for not its quality alone but also for the excitement the product can offer him. His buying experience should be delightful. It is always the perceived value of a product that matters.

Emotional buying

Human beings are emotional, they are sensitive and they will only do stuff that is programmed in their mind. In buying no amount of pressure can make him buy a product or service unless he is convinced about it.

It is a known fact that people get influenced by emotion than logic. 80% of decisions are made only because of emotional reasons, this is the reason why some brands sell more than others despite them being more expensive. Among the persons having the opportunity to influence decision-making is the salesperson, who gets ample opportunity to interact with the customer. Only a well-trained sales professional will be able to use this opportunity to his advantage. As sales professionals, we should be able to identify the emotional triggers of the buyers, their hidden needs, their influencers, and the strongest reason that will convince them to buy.

A good salesperson should have developed a very good eye for observation, only then he can identify those hidden buying signals. Besides experience observation gives the successful salesman the sixth sense, intuition on the timing of the sales closure.

Ego satisfaction

What is it that makes one person superior to another? It is nothing but his ability to influence. This ability might be because of the position he holds in society, his financial strength, the knowledge he possesses, and all the connections and contacts he holds at the right place. The dependability developed by the right person through his conviction on values is quite convincing.

Sports personnel and artists are influential because of their achievements in their respective fields, and the celebrity status that they achieve in the process. They have a very large fan following and this gives them the power to play the role of an influencer. The same logic applies to politicians and social workers because they work for society and their identity is associated with people support they have created for themselves.

An entrepreneur and a businessman are influencers because they have financial strength, their contribution to society in the form of job creation, giving opportunity for others, and the power they could generate through their business.

A professional can be highly influential too. A surgeon, a lawyer, or an author has the knowledge and skill to influence.
We have people in a high religious position capable of influencing the whole community, every word of theirs is considered golden by their followers.

There are villains too in the game of influence. These villains are mafia dons, dictators, and terrorists who control people by creating fear.

All those people who feel that they have the ability to influence others do carry ego with them, the more power they feel about their position the bigger is their ego, they cannot accept anything that would hurt that ego, Hitler committed suicide when he knew that he would be caught by the allied forces, we know what has happened to Saddam Hussein when he was captured, he was humiliated, his ego was shattered.

Ego is a feeling of superiority that people perceive about themselves. They like others to pamper this ego.

The interesting aspect is that everyone carries some element of ego within them, all that is needed to capture their attention is to recognize their ego and boost it.

A great salesman understands this and can close big orders by managing the customer's ego to their advantage.

Buy for need

Why do people buy things or why do they spend money for some good or service?

The reason for it is that they have a very solid urge to buy. Every individual buyer buys for a different reason, maybe utility of the product for his company, family, or a child or the possibility of gifting the product to someone dear.

A smart salesperson identifies the hidden urge of the buyer. Some sales professionals are capable enough to locate those hidden desires and create real demand for the product. Economists say desire plus the availability of money to fulfill the desire creates demand for a product/service.

They are good at making the customer walk through the mesmerizing path of the selling/purchasing process, where the need is created for the first time in the mind of the customer, this is further converted to want, then to a strong buying desire. The stronger the desire the faster is the buying.

Many companies float sales offer to tap this potential, many of us must have identified our needs only after some sales promotions prompted us to do so. A good sales professional should always be vigilant for clues of buying presented by his customers.

Buy for fun

Buying is a pleasurable experience for some, they prefer to buy from exclusive outlets to enjoy this feeling.

You must have come across some people who would do their shopping only from big malls and hypermarkets, they don't mind driving miles to a supermarket to buy small things, for them online purchase or home delivery is not fun.

The sellers are aware of such buyers and they create the environment to suit such clients, they create exclusive display stores with great ambiance to lure such customers. These customers do not mind paying a little more for this experience. They consider shopping as entertainment and they don't mind spending a couple of hours window shopping in large superstores before they decide to choose their products. Such customers need variety and they do not like to be disturbed by aggressive salesmen unless they seek help. It is difficult to manage such customers because many a time these customers are just enjoying at the stores.

They are intuitive buyers and could buy products they don't need. A good display or demonstration might attract them to the product. These customers are moody and sensitive to the salesman's behavior, they would not like too much help from the sales team because they wish to make their own decisions and want to take full control of their buying process. The sales professional should carefully observe such clients and should be readily available to help when they seek information. Most of the time these customers buy much more than they have planned for.

Addicted Buyer

Some buyers are emotionally attached to a particular brand and they would go to any extent to own it. The bond is very strong between search buyers with their brand; these brands become legends. Harley Davidson, Royal Enfield, Apple, Michael Jackson are a few such brands, which created an iconic image in the minds of their customers.

Brand loyalty is just because of this emotional bonding customers connect with the brand. It becomes a habit and some of these brands can never be replaced. I have seen people reading "The Hindu" the same brand of newspaper for ages. In some families, the habit is passed on from one generation to another. They would never change "The Hindu" even if competitors give them their products free of cost. Remember, the newspaper is a product that is different every day. Yet readers are attached to such products because of permanency in values they carry.

Personal toiletries are another group of products to which people are very brand loyal. They are so much attached to their brand that they would go without using any brand but would never use a substitute product.

It is these loyal customers who help create great product organizations. Brand and its loyalty are not created overnight. It takes great effort, long-term business strategies, and branding exercises for creating a brand image. This might have created passionate fans for the brand. We all know the strength of an organisation is the strength of its brand; Pepsi, Coke, McDonalds, Wal-Mart, Amazon, Google, are a few Legend Brands, these are not created overnight.

Customer is important

We all know that customer is the sole reason of any business, any organisation which focuses on products or services cannot think of its existence without its customers. Gone are the days when customers considered sellers as the boss of the business. Today every customer understands his value, competition too contributed to this awareness of the customer. Consumer-oriented legislation has played a big role in this. In our country, the Consumer Protection Act, 1986 has given five rights to the consumers, including the right to customer education!

Today's customers are well informed, and they know their rights, they want only the best of everything and that too at the lowest price. They are not willing to compromise on the quality of service or even on features in a product, because they know that they are in demand.

Competition is willing to pay any price to get new customers into their fold, you must have observed how Uber gives free rides to all its new customers when they installed the app on their mobiles. Uber also gave free rides to all those who referred this app to friends. Imagine the kind of expense Uber must have incurred on this campaign. Amazon and Flipkart have a special campaign period during which they offer big discounts to their online customers and prospects. Such a campaign is done to retain their existing customers and also to bring in online purchase behavior to first-time users of the portal.

Customers are no longer delighted with simple discounts alone, they might feel good when they are offered freebies. Customers now realise how important they are.

Qualified to Sell

Selling is a skill which can be learned, everyone is qualified to sell, if they have a product to sell or a service to offer which can be traded for something in return.

Any individual who is capable of offering his knowledge or skill like a baker, a gardener, consultant, tutor, etc. they are selling their services. We can say with authority is selling is not a profession which only a few learned sales persons alone can acquire. The moment we decide to take up a sales responsibility, there are a few things we need to be prepared with, and we should know everything about the product or service which we plan to sell. Our knowledge about them should be much more than that of our prospective customers; only then we will be able to convince them about our offer. We should know who the clients are; knowledge about the prospective customer is very important to plan our sales objective. Every product or service has a defined market; this knowledge is a must for a salesperson if he expects to succeed.

The price of the product is important. The salesperson should know the price of his product concerning that of the competing products. He should also be able to give a convincing reason about his product's price; only then the customer would buy his product. To qualify for sales, one should also acquire sufficient knowledge about the competition, and one should be able to convince one why he is the best.

Knowledge and salesman

To succeed in sales, academic qualification is always good, but it is the passion for the work that would qualify one to become a good salesman. Passion to meet people, passion to talk, passion to travel, all this should be supported with a strong conviction about the product or service, we are going to sell.

A good salesman is also a very good communicator. He knows how to communicate effectively and how to pitch his ideas to his customer and convince them.

Selling any product or service would require the salesman to be fully convinced of what he is selling. Conviction comes out of knowledge – knowledge of the product as well as similar products of competitors. Take the example of a life insurance agent. He shall have an in-depth knowledge of the insurance policy he proposes to sell. Also, he should know similar insurance plans of other life insurance companies, mutual fund investments, share and debenture investments, Unit Trust of India's products, exchange-traded funds, NSC, MIS, RD of Post Offices, gold bonds of the Government of India, investment in gold, etc. In-depth knowledge will enable him to talk with authority. It gives confidence to the salesman and receptivity for the prospect.

Take the case of a professional who is specialised in Mergers and Acquisitions of companies. His sales pitch can make deals worth several millions of rupees. Here knowledge required is about aspects of company's market valuation, management, production, marketing, financial aspects, HR, the legal framework of M&A, company's assets and liabilities, etc. Decision-making takes a long process – approval by the chief executive, Board, and General Body Meetings of the company and in some cases approval by the Registrar of Companies, in some cases the government and Courts. As the value of the product goes up the time taken for decision making would also go up. It would vary depending on the number of people involved in this process, the more technical a product/service is, the selling becomes a team activity with many people getting involved to manage the technical aspects of the product/service. For higher value products the sales team should be well equipped with all relevant information concerning the product or service vis-a-vis the competition.

Patience is an important element in high-value sales some sales processes can stretch to a few years; this is what we see in high-value deals.

The Canvas

Every sales call is a unique experience, when there is an interaction between the seller and the buyer, the seller identifies the buyer's need and he would be giving the solution to the buyer in the form of a product or service.

Perhaps the most important occasion in a sales process is the face-to-face interaction with the customer. This is a Junction where the sale and purchase decisions are made. The salesperson and his products are assessed by the buyer during such interaction.

The product, the service, and the commitment of the organisation are assessed in the face-to-face sales call. There must have been many letters, emails, or telephonic communications earlier. This one meeting will decide the fate of the sales.

The salesman is like an artist, painting on a canvas, here the canvas is in the mind of the customer. To make a sales call successful, the canvas has to be prepared before a sales pitch is made. All the communications through brochures, promotions, emails, or telephone provide opportunity to make this canvas.

While preparing the canvas, the sales team should make the customer aware of the product, identify their problems and challenges in their current situation. Map the product's features with the challenges, thus creating an interest in the mind of the buyer. If the sales involve only through physical interaction like with a walk-in customer or in a one-to-one sales call, the first task at hand of the salesperson is to make the customer receptive and to create an atmosphere of comfort, before the sales process is initiated.

No amount of selling skill can close a deal unless the prospective customer is prepared to accept what you have to offer him.

One has to consciously prepare the Canvas for an effective sales call to happen. There may be situations when the salesman may have to tell 'this product of ours may not suit your need'. This creates confidence in the salesman, which may result in larger sales later.

Trigger to Senses

Our decisions are influenced by our emotions. No one is rational. This applies to our buying decisions as well. when we buy, we expect that the product or service should offer the same amount of comfort or satisfaction, some buying decisions may not be able to create a great deal of satisfaction, but they do help in overcoming dissatisfaction or a challenging situation. Imagine you are in a desert and you are thirsty. There is only one shop there selling bottled water is priced at USD 20 this purchase may not be a happy experience, but you still buy because you are in a situation where you are left with no other option. Despite your buying this product at an exorbitant price, you are very much dissatisfied with the deal.

A good salesperson should always strive to give a satisfactory feel to all his customers. Only a satisfied customer will bring in more customers. One should try to build an emotional connection between the buyer and the product, the customer should be convinced about the deal or he would feel cheated, despite buying your product. In this case, paying

USD 20 for bottled water was very disappointing to the customer. Had the salesman convince the customer about the pain involved in carrying the water and storing it refrigerated in the middle of the desert and the money involved in maintaining the shop in a hostile environment. The customer would have been able to appreciate the service offered by the seller and he would be happy to pay such a high price for the product.

Buyer, Seller, and Product

Who/what is the most important element in a sales process? Is it the product or the customer or the seller?

As far as a customer (buyer) is concerned he values the product, he pays for the product, and expects the product to be of value for the money he has paid for. If we look deep into the transaction we will realize that the customer gives more importance to their own need. The product is only a tool to satisfy this need of theirs, a customer might be willing to go with an alternative product if he feels that the substitute is better in satisfying his need.

Imagine the customer is visiting a coffee shop and he's hungry. His need will be satisfied if his hunger is taken care of with a coffee and a cake. He might be willing to choose an alternate snack or drink if the shop is willing to offer a special discount.

This shows that the customer's need is primary in any sales call. Once this need is identified it becomes very easy for the salesperson to close the sale with proper alignment of the benefit of his product with that of the need of the customer. His product would help in satisfying the real need of the customer in a better way.

Remember, the solution what the salesman offers should be better than the one the customer is already using or planning to use.

Modern E Tools

In today's world, it would be foolish for a salesperson to avoid the Internet and social media. We are in an era of the Internet, we see a different buying pattern of the customers, they have various options available at their command to buy a product or service. Many young customers prefer online purchases and they believe in the convenience of buying from home, it also helps them to save a lot of time and money.

How can a product-based company make its product go alive online? We see this power of online buying behavior, with the mobile phones selling only on e-platforms; some even launch few models exclusively through online stores. This not only saves a lot of marketing expense, but they save on infrastructure and logistics.

Moreover, a lot of free promotions by the portal help the new brands to get noticed by their prospective customers.

Promotions through mobile or Internet platforms are a must for a brand to succeed in sales focusing on the younger generation. This is the place where all products are to be displayed. Any segment can be promoted directly to its target audience with the help of various artificial intelligence tools offered by the portals. Mobile Internet has made e-platforms all the stronger in influencing customers.

The online salesman is equally important as the physical salesperson on the ground.

The first date

Let's understand the importance of the first encounter with a customer. This is very vital in creating a sales-friendly environment.

The customer should accept the salesperson as somebody who is there to help him solve his problems. Most often the salesperson is interested in selling his product at any cost, and in the bargain, he would fit his product as a solution to the customer's problem even if it is a bad fit. Any product is like a shoe, it should be a perfect fit for the customer if not he will never be comfortable walking in it. He would always feel cheated by the over-enthusiastic salesperson. Some salesmen refuse to unearth the real problem of the customer and they try to project some other problem to the customer, which might not even be the reason why the customer chose to buy their product.

If the salesperson can do proper probing with the customer, with the right kind of questions he would be in a position to help his client better. The moment the salesperson begins to understand his role as a solution provider, his approach and his behavior would change. He would start to act like a consultant willing to help his client, the real professional would never try to sell irrelevant products to his customer. Such sales might bring you revenue but it would leave a bad taste behind, the first date should always project the salesperson as a helpful consultant.

Don't give them what you have

Business pressure is inevitable; this is what keeps a business moving forward. Unless there is sales pressure, business would stand still and competition would take away our customers. A successful sales team would never miss any opportunity to sell. This could sometimes become a double-edged sword; when the salesperson goes on board with their aggressive sales. This is a very unpleasant situation when the prospective customer tries to avoid the salesman. I recall how prospects use to avoid insurance agents because some of them do not know the art of giving comfort to the customer. They were trying to push their product despite the customer's lack of need. An ideal salesman would spend some time with the prospect and understand his requirement. He would also be able to guide the customer to a proper product. The knowledge of the salesman should create the need for the customer. Many a time customer may not be aware of such a need present for him unless it was convincingly shown by a professional through a proper interview. This is a stage when the professional moves from sales to marketing.

The challenge with a salesman under pressure is to sell, what he has with him. Even if the product does not suit the customers' needs, a skilled salesman can sell any product to the customer. It is because the customer was seemingly convinced by the salesman. His conviction may not last for long. The moment the customer realizes how he was made to buy a product, he never asked for, he feels cheated; this is the reason why many organizations do have a product-return-policy. This policy is to give the customer some amount of relief and protection against forced purchase.

Objections are welcome

In sales calls salesmen fear unpleasant questions put by some prospects/customers about the product or service; many opportunities are lost because of the unprepared salesmen.

The customer who objects to a sales pitch, with counter questions does not mean to offend the salesman, instead, he expects to be educated on all aspects of the product/service or after-sales service, service during the warranty period, etc. In an M&A negotiation quite unexpectedly the Company's official asked about the protection of the gratuity and pension liabilities of employees of the company that was being taken over and the M&A negotiator contacted over the telephone an expert on the subject (who was well-known to him) and gave all clarifications on the spot and made him speak to the expert. The deal was closed when answers were given with clarity. The query was not to offend the negotiator but for getting educated on the subject.

Customer's curiosity is reflected in objections to product features, the customer who asks too many questions is the one who is key to your sales. Product features must be projected as product benefits; herein lies the salesman's effectiveness.

Only a very knowledgeable salesman with understanding will be able to respond effectively to customers' queries. Knowledge, understanding, and attitude are the keywords.

Product knowledge is a must for any salesperson to address the various queries posed by prospects. Some of the doubts put forward by the customers might even help one identify new benefits of the product's usage. A salesperson should encourage prospective customers to speak because that one sales interaction will offer the opportunity to understand the customer's need and the sales person can use that information to increase his product's scope.

At times these customers would help the company in improving their products with additional features.

If every interaction were to result in a sale there was no need for salesmen. Some sales efforts may not be successful always, but remember, that does not comment adversely on the salesman.

Not to sell

Is it that the role of a salesman is only to sell? The sales manager is concerned with the ultimate result - the number of sales, more and more sales. This is true for all organisations working with selling/marketing.

It is a tough decision for a salesman to take, when he has to decline to sell a product to a prospective customer. Should he do that?

Sometimes we might come across customers, very enthusiastic about buying a product, which might be of no use to them; in such a situation despite having the product the salesperson should be bold enough to refuse the temptation of selling. He should use it as an opportunity to educate the customer as to why the product is not suitable for their kind of usage. Imagine you are selling as sewing machine design for home usage, these machines may be very good with features with advanced technology, a buyer who is an owner of a garment manufacturing unit is interested in buying 20 of your machines. In a garment manufacturing unit they work 24 hours in 3 shifts, and you know that your machines are not designed for heavy-duty. Should you sell them your product?

This could be a very difficult offer to refuse. A knowledgeable and committed salesperson would know that a machine designed for home use cannot be used for commercial purposes because the wear and tear of a commercial product are much more than that of a domestic one. Selling such a product to the manufacturer will be a disaster because the joy of selling 20 units would be gone the moment you start receiving breakdown complaints.

The ideal salesperson should make the customer aware of these challenges and suggest an alternate solution. Once the customer is educated about the problem, his respect for the salesperson would go up and the salesperson can also help the buyer in identifying a different product suitable for his needs. He rises to the level of a consultant.

A good salesperson never sells a wrong product to the right customer as it would destroy his reputation with one stroke.

Time management

Time is very precious ,every professional should be able to get maximum out of the available time.Proper planning is required for every activity ,only then one would be able to manage time effectively.Few tips to manage time are Start your day early,successful people start their work early.Set priorities and goals when planning your day,often people tend to spend valuable time on unimportant work.Focus on one task at a time,learn to delegate,it is always better to delegate work to others.Apply the 80/20 rule which means 80% of our time is spent on 20% of activities,Ensure that 20% is on priority list.Keep in some time for distractions and interruptions.Say no more often,you need not take up work when you have no time to do it, and master the art of short meetings,keep meetings short and to the point.

Energy in sales

Over-enthusiasm can kill a sale. One can be passionate about one's product, passion is a must to take a product forward, but one should also know to what extent one should project the passion before the client. It is because the prospect/customer does not share the same kind of enthusiasm about your product as the salesman does. Many prospects/customers view with suspicion excessive enthusiasm to sell.

The salesman may be genuinely interested in protecting the benefits of his product/service and what the prospect/customer gains by using his product, but it might backfire as the salesman's high energy in the product presentation might convey aggression. The buyer might assume it as pressure marketing. He may stay away from signing the dotted line.

A salesman was selling a handheld computer to a customer in Kuala Lumpur way back in 2003. This computer was a small handheld device and it was the first of its kind available in those days. He was very enthusiastic about the tough product. During a demo, the salesman was supposed to just tap the device on the desk to demonstrate its toughness, but instead, he hit it hard on the edge of the table and broke the display in front of the customer, it was very embarrassing, and that sale never materialized. The salesman was very confident about the product but his enthusiasm killed the sale. Only then did he realise how delicate the display screen is.

Some lessons are learned the hard way from such humiliating experiences. Never show your obsession or pressure to a customer.

Understand Trend

Successful people are those who are good at predicting the future. They can predict what is required for success tomorrow. Most people believe that the future is an extension of the present. It is never that way.

To be future-ready one should be very much aware of and conscious of all the little changes happening around us. Twenty years ago we could have never imagined that online sales would replace store sales. We know how foolish it would be to depend only on store sales. We should never discard futuristic ideas.

Driver-less cars and door delivery by drones were impossible yesterday but tomorrow these would be normal.

If we keenly observe we get the clues of the changing social and business trends and future taking shape around us. A progressive salesperson should take cues from this and he should be able to develop products and services keeping the future in mind.

The sales focused organisations will be future-ready; they should be able to think ahead of the competition. The successful ones will survive others will wither away. Their sales-men's future cannot be different!

The customer expectations

Every customer is special. He should be taken care of always by the company. Unfortunately once a sale is closed, the customer is handled by the delivery department, their understanding of the customer's need is based only on the information the sales team shared with them.

It is often found that the customer's expectations were different from what is delivered to him by the production team. It is because there was no proper documentation of the customer's need and the same have not been rightly conveyed to the production department. When there is no proper mapping of the customer's requirement with the product's features one will end up creating a dissatisfied customers.

Proper hand-holding is a must when the products are customised as per individual requirements. The salesperson should always be part of the delivery team. Confusion of deliverable is often seen with intangible service products like ERP software solutions. The need keep changing as the implementation progress. This creates avoidable misunderstanding and big revenue loss. The customer would never agree to pay more for the changes they requested before the product is delivered whereas the production team must have already completed the product development. In such a scenario any change in the specification would require a big investment. This is where the negotiation skill of the salesperson should be put to use. we may not satisfy every customer always, but proper documentation of the customer requirement can eliminate conflicts to some extent.

It is always better if we can plan to deliver something more than what is committed.

Door to Door Selling

A frustrating experience for a prospect/customer is meeting an uninvited salesman, who unexpectedly gate-crashed into his house. The prospective customer would usually close his mind from receiving any new information. He becomes a tough nut to crack.

Why do people behave like this to an innocent salesman? There could be so many reasons as to why the prospect behaved the way he did?

People do have their own choices and preference as regards utilisation of their time. No one likes intrusion into his privacy.

A salesman's unannounced visit might have made the prospect uncomfortable, he must have been doing something important, or the visit must have upset his planned schedule or he might not consider the salesman credible enough to spend his time listening. Whatever might be the reason, if the salesperson is unable to get an interview with the prospect, the sales call will never progress to the next level.

The important duty of a salesperson is to make the customer comfortable and willing to listen to his sales story. There should be an element of curiosity and credibility in what he says. How he says is more important than what he says. The first 20 seconds a salesman spends with the customer will determine the fate of the next 20 minutes of the meeting.

A good public relations activity by the organisation might create a positive image about the company in the mind of the customer. People only prefer to meet someone with whom they are comfortable. At least they should be able to connect with the product or service or on a personal level.

Much of the effort should be focused on creating a warm environment to begin the sales process, once that is done, the road ahead will be smooth.

Industrial Selling

Selling complex and sophisticated industrial and engineering products is more difficult compared to selling a non-technical product.

In industrial selling, the customers are usually high-value customers and their buying cycle is also big. There would be many departments involved in the purchase. Usually, the users are not the buyers.

If the organisation is a production-based company, the requirement of the product might be a part of their raw material and their purchase decision is made by a team, e.g. experts from production, quality assurance, finance, and materials departments jointly decide. There may be many vendors identified and short-listed after proper evaluation of the product as well as various pre-defined parameters, like quality specifications, price specifications, past supplier history, existing clients etc..

The sales team, not the salesman alone, should be very active while selling to large organisations. Since the process is time-consuming, involves thousands of dollars, and is highly technical, it requires patience and proper connections with various influencers. These relationships help the salesperson in taking the process forward.

Take the example of selling refractory bricks to a steel plant.
The competition is very tough in high-value sales and in most cases senior management gets involved in the negotiation process. The sales team should be able to guide the management in their pricing, payment, and delivery strategy, with timely sharing of information about the buyer requirement and completion strategies.

Thorough knowledge and negotiation skill with good market intelligence alone can help in successful industrial selling. The salesperson should also be able to understand the capability of his organisation to deliver, since most of the high-value sales begin with strong conditionalities attached, like the penalty clause on bad delivery.

Reading the fine lines in the contract is a must, to avoid surprises at a later date.

FMCG selling

In FMCG selling is more of indirect selling, the buyer is not the user. A salesperson should be focusing on retail availability and visibility of products at various outlets.

A typical day starts with a travel plan, wherein the salesman makes a list of customers he plans to meet, and the best route to reach them all. He is supposed to carry an Order book, the latest price list, and the company's offers/schemes circulars which would be used to inform retailers and dealers. Most of these are digitally managed in big organisations through ERP software. Smaller companies still depend on physical methods.

The salesman is also supposed to ensure that the selected retail outlet participates in different promotional activities. He is also responsible for proper product display at each store.

Nothing speaks louder than numbers. For any salesman to become successful he should ensure that his targets are not compromised.

His sales objectives are to be met through his distributors and stockiests. They play a very vital role in FMCG/pharmaceutical business. A good relationship with the supply chain is essential to becoming successful in this role. There should be total control on the distributor retailer product flow. Availability of products at the shelf can only bring sales because whatever marketing activity the company plans, it is the availability and visibility at the retailer that yields sales volume. It is the biggest challenge for the sales team to ensure retail space;

every competitor will fight for the best visible space on the retail shelf. Many retailers sell display space which has to be monitored and managed by the sales team. In big stores, some organisations depute sales promoters to get a better and bigger volume of business.

At each distributor, van sales boys are appointed to pick up sales orders from retailers. This arrangement is very helpful to support sales where there is no exclusive distributor. Van sales system is very useful to have better market control.

For a successful FMCG business, there should be proper synchronization of sales, marketing, and logistics departments. The sales professional ensures good control over this system.

Pharmaceutical Selling

Medical detail man was a term used for pharmaceutical sales professionals long ago. In his book, "strong medicine" Arthur Hailey has very clearly told the story of a pharmaceutical company executive and his work, which was the kind of Pharmaceutical sales business in the 70s.

Pharma selling is one of the most challenging jobs, this involves very strong knowledge of chemistry, pharmacy, human anatomy&physiology, and marketing. The most important element is updating knowledge to keep pace with the introduction of each molecule by the industry. A pharmaceutical sales executive or the medical representative has to undergo regular training on new developments in the product, market place, and industry, unlike other industries, the sales executive here has no direct contact with the end-user. The customer is never the user of the product.

The doctor who is the customer of the pharmaceutical company only prescribes the product to his patients. Stockists and medical stores take the medicine to the end consumer. These patients pay for the product and use drugs as advised by the physician.

The doctor's confidence in the product is what decides his prescription. Most of pharmaceutical Companies try to convince doctors about their products. They bombard doctors with many kinds of literature and case study reports, to give them enough confidence to prescribe. Doctors are given free samples, to try the products and to be convinced about their efficacy.

We at times never understand why a doctor request sample of a well-tested and established molecule? Why should the doctor require samples of Ranitidine or Ampicillin or Diclofenac sodium all these molecules are been prescribed for more than 30 years now and what additional trial or test is that doctor is going to do with these samples? Yet pharmaceutical companies shower doctors with physician samples.

Many companies started restricting free samples and they would supply them only on request.

Doctors are the pampered lot of the pharmaceutical companies; some doctors are given gifts, books, sponsorship to conferences by few pharmaceutical companies to ensure continuous prescription of their products.

Hospital stores too play an important role in prescriptions. These medical representatives have to get the doctor's support in the form of prescriptions and at the same time need to convince the retail shops and the hospital stores-in-charge to keep sufficient inventory of the products. Companies float various schemes and offer to make sure that the stocks are maintained in medical shops and stores.

The pharmaceutical salesperson has a bigger role to play than just product promotion. Public relations activities are to be regularly conducted as a part of his company's policy, like free medical camps and seminars. In short, they are the event managers for their companies and tour planners of the doctors when they are out for conferences.

The sole responsibility of the Pharmaceutical sales professional is to ensure that the medical fraternity is taken care of and the system is well oiled to generate maximum prescriptions for their products in a highly technical and competitive scenario.

Dealer sales

Automobile and furniture dealers have a salesman who remains technically sound with fire in their belly. They have to be very vigilant to understand each customer's aspirations and their needs; they will be able to guide the customers into buying their products.

A car salesman observes the customers and the full family understands the role of each member of the family in the buying process. The person who is spending the money may not be the person who decides on the purchase. A teenage son or daughter might be the influencer in this purchase. The father will be spending the money, whereas the Purchase Decision is done by others. The smart salesman focuses his effort on convincing the influencer about the various features and advantages of the car. A vigilant salesman can influence the right person and he may be able to sell a higher variant of the product to the influencer.

Most of the customers know as information is available freely. Many buyers come well prepared with all the information about the product from various sources even before they visit the showroom or dealer.

The salesman, in such situations, should make the prospective customer experience the product, and if it is a car the comfort of the ride should be made available to the buyer and his family. The family is given a ride in the car which is neat cool and fresh with the smell of fragrance, this will influence the final buying decision.

The salesman ensures that he gives due importance to each member of the family, who came to buy the car and he can address the need of each influencer. If even one of the family members decides against your product you might lose that business.

Another challenge with a salesman is that he should on many occasions manage the financing of the purchase, exchange old furniture or vehicle with a new one. These companies may have a policy to help in buying back used cars or furniture. Many people are reluctant to buy because they find it difficult disposing of the old used stuff. The sales organisation should address this challenge and it will bring in many new buyers.

There should be a proper follow-up system in dealer sales, the sales team should be able to keep in touch with all those customers who had visited the showroom. Higher value purchase is never made with a single visit alone, people may pay multiple visits to the showroom and competitors before they sign on the dotted line.

BB Matrix- The Buyer Behaviour

Prospects can be classified into four categories, Diamond, Power Horse, Champion & Deep Mine. Let us look at each type of prospective buyer separately and try to understand their buying behaviour and strategies which an organisation should adopt to capture these customers.

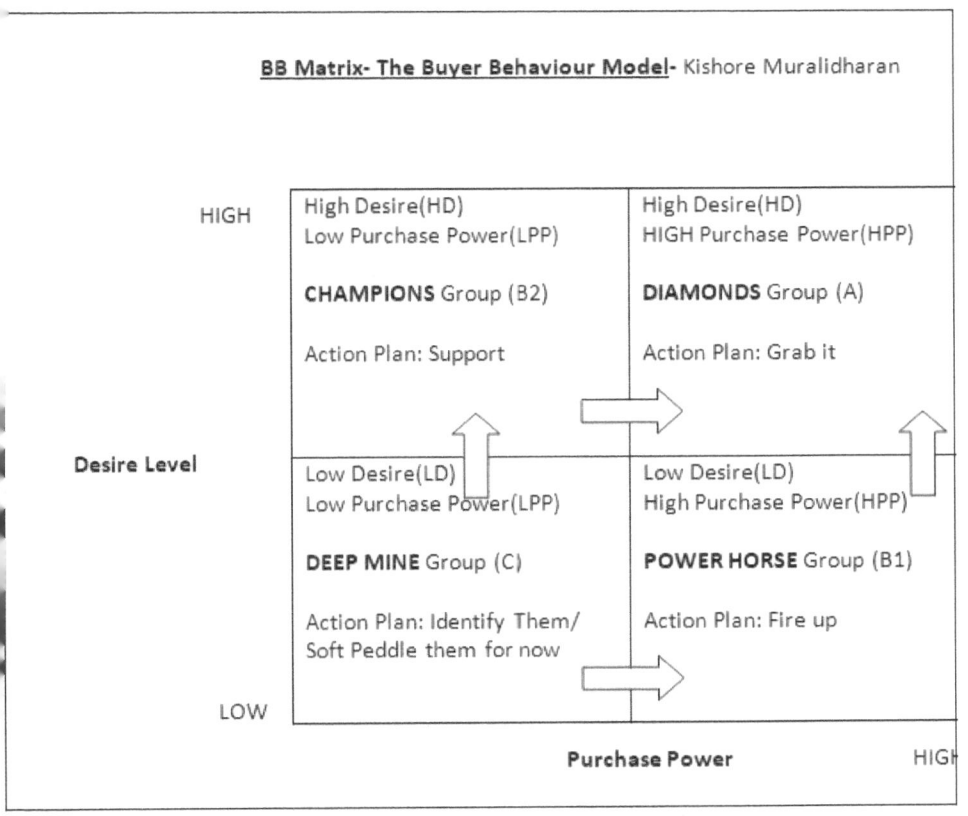

Diamonds

Diamonds, they fall under Group (A) category of prospects. They have
High Desire & High Purchase Power, The action plan an organisation should adopt is a) Grab them/Catch them, b)Meet them, c)Be with them till they buy from you. They require high focus approach.
Diamond have high desire and high purchasing power. The resource focus should be very high and at the same time urgency focus should also be the priority. This is the ideal scenario where the company should grab the opportunity and get the business from the prospect using all available resources at their disposal.
For example, a family visiting a car showroom or a jewellery shop is ideal situation where the buyer is very much prepared to purchase and at the same time they are financially ready to make a decision. The sole purpose of visiting a silk sarees showroom or jewellery shop itself is an indication of high desire and high purchase power of the customer. The strategy should be to use the best salesperson available and ensure that the purchases are made. If organisations miss out on this customer, these customers might go elsewhere to fulfill their desire of purchase. Some of the examples
 1. Enquiry at an academic institution..
 2. Direct visit by a customer to shop or a showroom.
 3. Customer at beauty salon.
 4. Patient visiting a hospital.

No strategy is foolproof, and every Diamond customer might not respond in the same fashion, there could be exceptions and various other factors influencing their decisions are to be measured and plan of action should be designed accordingly.

Power Horse

POWER HORSE they form Group (B1) with Low Desire & High Purchase Power.The
Action Plan should be to Fire up their desire with right kind of promotional strategies ,educating them about the product and service.Medium term focus approach.

Here the desire level is low and purchase power is high, the resource focus should be calculated,whereas urgency focus should also be given equal importance as resource. We put both under the B1 group.

In most cases the buyer in this quadrant has not yet decided to buy the product or service but he or she has the purchasing power to decide. Reason of low desire could be because their need is not yet identified. This is the main role of the organisation, the marketing team and the sales team should focus on need creation.

This is always done for a new product launch .For example if a new restaurant or a new vehicle is launched the prospects are identified based on their purchasing power and promotional activities are targeted towards them. The resource focus & urgency is high at B1 quadrant. Urgency is similar to quadrant B2 that is champions.

The action plan for the power horse is to fire up the desire. The organisation should do everything to achieve this objective, that would move the customer from being a PowerHorse to a diamond.

UBER & Swiggy offered a lot of freebies and conducted many campaigns to get people to use their products. Uber offered 5 free rides to anybody who registered with them, they also offered free rides for referral. Swiggy the app based food delivery company gave flat 50% discounts to all new users.

No strategy is foolproof, and every PowerHorse customer might not respond in the same fashion, there could be exceptions and various other factors influencing their decisions are to be measured and plan of action should be designed accordingly. The objective should be to move PowerHorse to become Diamond.

Urgency focus and Resource focus should be very similar in both B1 & B2 groups, the balancing act is to be played by the management depending on organisational strategy and priority.

Champions

Champions fall under Group (B2)
High Desire &Low Purchase Power,Here the action plan is to support this group, because they are already sold on your product /service.
Here the desired level is high and the purchase power is low. Resource focus is at B and urgency focus is also at B.
These are the prospects who have high desire yet are unable to purchase the product or service because of lack of financial power. Champions are good promoters of the products or service because they are already convinced above the product or service and they would play the role of a good influencer for promoting the product to others , even though they are unable to own them.
For example young men just out of college are crazy about super bikes but their income is insufficient to buy such bikes. They understand its benefits and they are willing to pay for your product, but they lack buying power.This group can be a good ambassador for the product/brand. Harley Davidson is promoted by millions of champions.
The best strategy for the organisation is to support them through easy EMI or special referral schemes.
Eg. I Phones, Royal Enfield Bullet.

These products have many diehard fans willing to promote these products to their friends and relatives who can buy.

No strategy is fool proof, and every Champion customer might not respond to marketing stimuli in the same fashion, there could be exceptions and various other factors influencing their decisions are to be measured and a plan of action should be designed accordingly. The objective should be to move Champions to become Diamonds.

Urgency focus and Resource focus should be very similar in both B1 & B2 groups, the balancing act is to be played by the management depending on organisational strategy and priority.

Deep Mine

Deep Mine can be called group (C)
Low Desire & Low Purchase Power. Here action plan should be to Identify them/soft pedal for now, this group could be the future prospects and it is always better to
earmark a small promotional budget for this group. Let's remember that dead logs too can grow mushrooms under the right conditions.
Many educational institutions design strategies to reach out to their future prospects through seminars and organising competitions at high school levels.

Eg: Lakysha an CA coaching institute from Kerala,India conduct quiz programs for high school students, though these students will take 2 more years to qualify as prospects.

JCI, an international NGO conducts many empowering youth programs for school students ,so that these students can experience Jaycees and can become future members of the organisation once they turn 18.No strategy is foolproof, and every Deep Mine prospect might not respond in the same fashion, there could be exceptions and various other factors influencing their decisions are to be measured and a plan of action should be designed accordingly. The objective should be to move Deep Mine to become either Champions or Power Horse.